Made in United States
Troutdale, OR
08/20/2023

12219083R00084